On Being a Friend

For most of us, acquaintances come into our lives in droves. Many of them generally remain little more than people on the periphery of our lives, warranting a quick smile or a brief "hello," or they almost immediately move on, leaving at best a vague recollection. And as much as we may love — and even *like* — our relatives, as the old expression goes, we don't get to choose them; they come as a package at birth.

Friends, however, are altogether another matter. Friends come of their own free will, for reasons that make perfect sense and for reasons that often seem baffling. With some of our friends, we may have so much in common that we seem carbon copies of one another. Other friends may be our polar opposites in everything from musical taste to political leanings. But all true friends have one trait in common: They stick by us through thick and thin, good times and bad. To paraphrase James Taylor, when you need them, they'll be there.

The concept of friendship has been examined for as long as humans have been putting pen to paper — or, for that matter, chisels to clay tablets or ink to parchment. The ancients had varying opinions on the subject. In 3000 B.C., a Sumerian philosopher recorded a cuneiform axiom for posterity: "Friendship lasts a day; kinship lasts forever."

In other words: Blood is thicker than water. Apparently that unknown scribe had never experienced the joy of true friendship.

The ancient Greeks and Romans also took up the idea of friendship. In 350 B.C., the Greek philosopher Aristotle (384 B.C.–322 B.C.) examined friendship at length in Book VIII of his *Nicomachean Ethics*. However, his understanding of friendship was essentially one of obligatory reciprocity with three elements: usefulness, pleasure, and respect for character. Emotions didn't seem to play much of a role.

It wasn't until a few centuries later that the great Roman poet/philosopher/orator Marcus Tullius Cicero (106 B.C.–43 B.C.) recognized, and expounded on, the importance of friendship as something central to our lives for reasons of affection and emotional intimacy. As Cicero pointed out, *amicitia*, the Latin word for friendship, is derived from the Latin *amor,* or love, "and love is certainly the prime mover in contracting mutual affection." His treatise *On Friendship* stands as an ageless testimonial to abiding, important relationships and how vital they are to happiness.

In this book, you'll find musings on friends and friendship by authors, philosophers, and just plain folks from ancient times to the present day. May you — and your dearest friends — find inspiration, affirmation, entertainment, and even a bit of enlightenment within these pages.

A friend is one who walks in when others walk out.

— Walter Winchell

Friendship, Friendship,
Just the Perfect Blendship . . .

C ole Porter had a wonderful definition for friendship. But how is friendship usually defined? *Merriam-Webster's Collegiate Dictionary* states that a friend is "one who is attached to another by affection or esteem; a favored companion" and defines friendship simply as "the state of being friends." But anyone who has ever had a true friend knows that the relationship goes far beyond those succinct words. Cicero urged his fellow Romans to "regard friendship as the greatest thing in the world; for there is nothing which so fits in with our nature, or is so exactly what we want in prosperity or adversity . . . Friendship is the only thing in the world concerning the usefulness of which all mankind is agreed."

Since Cicero's time, of course, countless others have authored thoughts on the meaning of friendship. Some have compared friendship with the other significant relationships in our lives and acknowledged the uniqueness of this bond. No matter what their words, all of these authors agree that friendship is essential to life.

[W]ith the exception of wisdom, I am inclined to think nothing better than this has been given to man by the immortal gods . . . What can be more delightful than to have someone to whom you can say everything with the same absolute confidence as to yourself? Is not prosperity robbed of half its value if you have no one to share your joy?

— Marcus Tullius Cicero

Friendship is by its very nature freer of deceit than any other relationship we can know because it is the bond least affected by striving for power, physical pleasure, or material profit, most liberated from any oath of duty or of constancy.

— Francine du Plessix Gray, *Friendship*

The feeling of friendship is like that of being comfortably filled with roast beef, love, like being enlivened with champagne.

— Samuel Johnson

Friendship always benefits; love sometimes injures.

— Lucius Annaeus Seneca the Younger

Friendships are different from all other relationships. Unlike acquaintanceship, friendship is based on love. Unlike lovers and married couples, it is free of jealousy. Unlike children and parents, it knows neither criticism nor resentment. Friendship has no status in law. Business partnerships are based on a contract. So is marriage. Parents are bound by law. But friendships are freely entered into, freely given, and freely exercised.

— Stephen Ambrose

Friendship maketh indeed a fair day in the affections, from storm and tempests; but it maketh daylight in the understanding, out of darkness and confusion of thoughts.

— Francis Bacon

The essence of friendship is entireness, a total magnanimity and trust.

— Ralph Waldo Emerson

Friendship is almost always the union of a part of one mind with a part of another.

— George Santayana

Love is blind; friendship closes its eyes.

— Anonymous

Friendship is the source of the greatest pleasures.

— St. Thomas Aquinas

The language of friendship is not words but rather meanings. It is an intelligence above language.

— Henry David Thoreau

I always felt that the great high privilege, relief, and comfort of friendship was that one had to explain nothing.

— Katherine Mansfield

The glory of friendship is not the outstretched hand, nor the kindly smile nor the joy of companionship; it is the spiritual inspiration that comes to one when he discovers that someone else believes in him and is willing to trust him.

— Ralph Waldo Emerson

Friendship with oneself is all-important because without it, one cannot be friends with anyone else in the world.

— Eleanor Roosevelt

 Special Handling Required

When we find ourselves taking new forks in the road of life, friendships often need special nurturing. When one of you marries, has a child, or gets a job that demands long hours and lots of travel, and the other stays single, childless, or office bound, it may take extra effort — and some creative planning — to stay connected. If you want your friendship to last, do whatever it takes. Sign up for a class together, take the baby for walks together, drive your friend to the airport and have coffee before her flight.

Friendship is a horizon that expands whenever we approach it.

— E. R. Hazlip

Friendship needs no words — it is solitude delivered from the anguish of loneliness.

— Dag Hammarskjöld

It is a sweet thing, friendship, a dear balm,
A happy and auspicious bird of calm. . . .

— Percy Bysshe Shelley

Friendship is a sheltering tree.

— Samuel Taylor Coleridge

The other element of friendship is tenderness. We are beholden to men by every sort of tie — by blood, by pride, by fear, by hope, by lucre, by lust, by hate, by admiration, by every circumstance and badge and trifle — but we can scarce believe that so much character can subsist in another as to draw us by love.

— Ralph Waldo Emerson

Friendship is constant in all other things,
Save in the office and affairs of love.

— William Shakespeare

Friendship is the only cement that will ever hold the world together.

— Woodrow Wilson

There can be no friendship when there is no free-dom. Friendship loves the free air and will not be fenced up in straight and narrow enclosures.

— William Penn

Many a time from a bad beginning great friendships have sprung up.

— Publius Terentius Afer (Terence)

My careful heart was free again, —
O friend, my bosom said,
Through thee alone the sky is arched,
Through thee the rose is red.

— Ralph Waldo Emerson

Friendship consists in forgetting what one gives and remembering what one receives.

— Alexandre Dumas the Younger

I keep my friends as misers do their treasure because of all the things granted us by wisdom, none is greater or better than friendship.

— Pietro Aretino

The holy passion of friendship is of so sweet and steady and loyal and enduring a nature that it will last through a whole lifetime — if not asked to lend money.

— Mark Twain

Friendship is the union of spirits, a marriage of hearts, and the bond there of virtue.

— Samuel Johnson

He whose hand is clasped in friendship cannot throw mud.

— Proverb

The worst solitude is to be destitute of sincere friendship.

— Francis Bacon

The best mirror is an old friend.

— Irish proverb

Ya Gotta Have Friends . . .

Friends reflect who we are and who we hope to be. Sometimes our friends are the better part of us. Sometimes we are the better part of them. A friend can unburden a heart and help a soul to sing. A friend is someone who feels like home. Friendship is, in fact, the solid core of every emotionally intimate relationship. As the Greek philosopher Aristotle noted c. 350 B.C., "Without friends, no one would want to live, even if he had all other goods."

Without friends, even the most agreeable pursuits become tedious.

— St. Thomas Aquinas

A faithful friend is the medicine of life.

— Ecclesiaticus 6:16 (Apocrypha)

Life has no blessing like a prudent friend.

— Euripides

A man cannot be said to succeed in this life who does not satisfy one friend.

— Henry David Thoreau

Who finds a faithful friend finds a treasure.

— Jewish proverb

Life is partly what we make it and partly what is made by the friends whom we choose.

— Tehyi Hsieh

Tell me what company thou keepst, and I'll tell thee what thou art.

— Miguel de Cervantes

A friend is one to whom one may pour out all the contents of one's heart, chaff and grain together, knowing that the gentlest of hands will take and sift it, keep what is worth keeping, and with a breath of kindness blow the rest away.

— Arabian proverb

A friend may well be reckoned the masterpiece of nature.

— Ralph Waldo Emerson

Nothing makes the earth so spacious as to have friends at a distance.

— Henry David Thoreau

A true friend unbosoms freely, advises justly, assists readily, adventures boldly, takes all patiently, defends courageously, and continues a friend unchangeably.

— William Penn

A friend is someone who reaches for your hand but touches your heart.

— Antoine de Saint Exupéry

It is one of the blessings of old friends that you can afford to be stupid with them.

— Ralph Waldo Emerson

Friends are an aid to the young, to guard them from error; to the elderly, to attend to their wants and to supplement their failing power of action; to those in the prime of life, to assist them to noble deeds.

— Aristotle

A friend is a gift you give yourself.

— Robert Louis Stevenson

Friends find comfort in what they share and delight in how they differ.

— Anonymous

No soul is desolate as long as there is a human being for whom it can feel trust and reverence.

— George Eliot

Friends have all things in common.

— Plato

It is a curious thing in human experience, but to live through a period of stress and sorrow with another person creates a bond that nothing seems able to break.

— Eleanor Roosevelt

A friend is, as it were, a second self.

— Marcus Tullius Cicero

My friends are my estate.

— Emily Dickinson

One loyal friend is worth ten thousand relatives.

— Euripides

A friend is someone who doesn't like the same people you do.

— Proverb

A friend is a person who knows all about you — and still likes you.

— Elbert Hubbard

A friend is a person with whom I may be sincere. Before him, I may think aloud.

— Ralph Waldo Emerson

It takes a long time to grow an old friend.

— John Leonard

First Friends

Think about your childhood friends. How those first friendships shape you and sustain you during your formative years — and your angst-ridden teens. The friends who come to us in the springtime of our lives stay with us forever, whether they're literally with us as we go through life or only lodged deep in memory. Meet up with an old friend at a high-school reunion thirty years later, and on one level it's as if there has been no passage of time. You may no longer be the same person — indeed, everything about you except your first name may have changed — but even if your paths have never crossed in all the intervening years, that connection remains, as if protected in a time capsule. More often than not, as soon as the reunion ends, so too does the briefly reawakened friendship. Yet in a very real sense, that bond will remain strong for the whole of your life.

O playmate in the golden time!
Our mossy seat is green,
Its fringing violets blossom yet,
The old trees o'er it lean.

— John Greenleaf Whittier, "My Playmate"

There is magic in the memory of schoolboy friendships; it softens the heart and even affects the nervous system of those who have no heart.

— Benjamin Disraeli

[The] companions of our childhood always possess a certain power over our minds which hardly any later friend can obtain.

— Mary Wollstonecraft Shelley

[N]o matter how old you are, when you go out into the world, it is best to hold hands and stick together.

— Robert Fulghum

From the rocking horse to the rocking chair, friendship keeps teaching us about being human.

I'll Be On Your Side
Forever More . . .

Because, as Burt Bacharach knows, that's what friends are for. Deep, abiding friendships are a source of great joy. They can also seem quite magical. How did such a connection happen? What was it that formed such a strong bond, despite outward differences? With best friends we find a warm glow and an easy comfort. There is no need for small talk, for explanations of who we are, what we do, or where we're going. In fact, there is often no need for words at all — we can spend hours on end simply being in each other's company. Even sudden separation has no impact; we're still best friends, despite communicating only via telephone and e-mail. A great friendship may be the equivalent of an alchemist's transmutation of lead into gold, for true friends can change us in profound ways, enabling us to see things in ourselves that we might never discover without their guidance.

No receipt openeth the heart but a true friend, to whom you may impart griefs, joys, fears, hopes, suspicions, counsels, and whatsoever lieth upon the heart to oppress it, in a kind of civil shrift or confession.

— Francis Bacon

When a man becomes dear to me, I have touched the goal of fortune.

— Ralph Waldo Emerson

Each friend represents a world in us, a world possibly not born until they arrive, and it is only by this meeting that a new world is born.

— Anaïs Nin

Friendship is one mind in two bodies.

— Meng Tzu

When true friends meet in adverse hour,
'Tis like a sunbeam through a shower.
A watery way an instant seen,
The darkly closing clouds between.

— Sir Walter Scott

Think where man's glory most begins and ends,
And I say my glory was I had such friends.

— William Butler Yeats

For memory has painted this perfect day
With colors that never fade,
And we find at the end of a perfect day
The soul of a friend we've made.

— Carrie Jacobs Bond

Faithful friends are beyond price: No amount can balance their worth.

— Sirach 6:15

Friendship requires that rare mean betwixt likeness and unlikeness, that piques each with the presence of power and of consent in the other party.

— Ralph Waldo Emerson

This communicating of a man's self to his friend works two contrary effects, for it redoubleth joy and cutteth grief in half.

— Francis Bacon

There is nothing on this earth to be prized more than true friendship.

— St. Thomas Aquinas

Friendship that flows from the heart cannot be frozen by adversity, as the water that flows from the spring cannot congeal in winter.

— James Fenimore Cooper

My only sketch, profile, of Heaven is a large blue sky . . . larger than the biggest I have seen in June — and in it are my friends, every one of them.

— Emily Dickinson

The most beautiful thing we can experience is the mysterious. It is the true source of art, science, and friendship.

— Albert Einstein

Friendship is never established as an understood relation. It is a miracle which requires constant proofs. It is an exercise of the purest imagination and of the rarest faith!

— Henry David Thoreau

Keep Spring in Your Friendship

Remember all the adventures you shared with your best friend when you were young? Well, keep it up! Your best friend now may be a different person, but you should resolve to have new adventures together every so often. Take a trip to someplace neither of you has ever been, explore, and have a picnic. Learn a new sport or hobby together. Or simply check out that new restaurant you've been hearing about. And here's the best part: Keeping your friendship nimble by engaging in new pursuits also keeps your mind nimble — another priceless gift the two of you can share.

What is a friend? A single soul in two bodies.

— Aristotle

When two people are at one in their inmost hearts,
They shatter even the strength of iron or of bronze.
And when two people understand each other in their inmost hearts,
Their words are sweet and strong, like the fragrance of orchids.

— I Ching
Great Commentary 1.8.6

Friendship should be more than biting Time can sever.

— T. S. Eliot

There is no distance too great between friends for love gives wings to the heart.

— Anonymous

The soul environs itself with friends that it may enter into a grander self-acquaintance or solitude; and it goes alone for a season that it may exalt its conversation or society.

— Ralph Waldo Emerson

I count myself in nothing else so happy
As in a soul rememb'ring my good friends.

— William Shakespeare

Friendship without self-interest is one of the rare and beautiful things in life.

— James Francis Byrnes

Friendship, like the immortality of the soul, is too good to be believed.

— Ralph Waldo Emerson

The making of friends who are real friends is the best token we have of a man's success in life.

— Edward Everett Hale

You Just Call
Out My Name . . .

Perhaps no song is recent memory so captures the spirit and substance of true friendship as "You've Got A Friend" by Carole King. And no doubt many of us have thought (or sung) those words when we've been "down and troubled and . . . need a helping hand" or have thought of friends in need and promised, "all you have to do is call and I'll be there." But friendship requires diligence, attentiveness, nurturing. Friendship is reciprocal and requires that the needs of both parties be met. Friends can't be taken for granted. Having a friend means being a friend.

Hold a true friend with both your hands.

— Nigerian proverb

I do not wish to treat friendships daintily but with the roughest courage. When they are real, they are not glass threads or frost-work but the solidest thing we know.

— Ralph Waldo Emerson

There is a miracle called friendship that dwells within the heart.

— Anonymous

The first law of friendship is that it has to be culti-
vated. The second law is to be indulgent when the first law
has been neglected.

— Voltaire

If we would build on a sure foundation in friendship, we must love friends for their sake rather than for
our own.

— Charlotte Brontë

Friendship, like love, is destroyed by long absence,
though it may be increased by short intermissions.

— Samuel Johnson

A friend loves at all times.

— Proverbs 17:17

Never injure a friend, even in jest.

— Marcus Tullius Cicero

We do not so much need the help of our friends as the confidence of their help in need.

— Epicurus

A friend should be a master at guessing and keeping still.

— Friedrich Nietzsche

Keep your friendships in repair.

— Ralph Waldo Emerson

Never deceive a friend.

— Hipparchus

In the sweetness of friendship, let there be laughter and sharing of pleasures.

— Kahlil Gibran

He who has a thousand friends has not a friend to spare.

— Ai Ibn-Abu-Talib

That friendship may be at once fond and lasting, there must not only be equal virtue on each part but virtue of the same kind; not only the same end must be proposed but the same means must be approved by both.

— Samuel Johnson

 Two (or More) Heads Are Better Than One

For many people, the autumn of their lives brings an urge for a new direction, a feeling that the work they've been doing — or the life they've been leading — somehow doesn't work anymore. If that sentence describes one of your friends, invite him over for a brainstorming session. Get some good wine and order the best pizza in town. Then call a few other creative thinkers and ask them to show up with Rolodexes in hand. Who knows? It could be the evening that launches a new career.

Laughter is the shortest distance between two people.

— Victor Borge

Go often to the house of thy friend for weeds choke the unused path.

— Ralph Waldo Emerson

True friendship ought never conceal what it thinks.

— St. Jerome

An honest answer is the sign of true friendship.

— Proverbs 18:24

When we seek to discover the best in others, we somehow bring out the best in ourselves.

— William Arthur Ward

Promises may get friends, but 'tis performance that keeps them.

— Benjamin Franklin

To let friendship die away by negligence and silence is certainly not wise. It is voluntarily to throw away one of the greatest comforts of the weary pilgrimage.

— Samuel Johnson

Don't walk in front of me, I may not follow.
Don't walk behind me, I may not lead.
Walk beside me and be my friend.

— Albert Camus

Anybody can sympathize with the sufferings of a friend, but it requires a very fine nature to sympathize with a friend's success.

— Oscar Wilde

The happiest moments my heart knows are those in which it is pouring forth its affections to a few esteemed characters.

— Thomas Jefferson

Much of the vitality in a friendship lies in the honoring of differences, not simply in the enjoyment of similarities.

— James Fredericks

The most I can do for my friend is simply to be his friend.

— Henry David Thoreau

Advice is like snow: The softer it falls, the longer it dwells upon, and the deeper it sinks into the mind.

— Samuel Taylor Coleridge

We must have infinite faith in each other.

— Henry David Thoreau

True friendship is never serene.

— Marie de Rabutin-Chantal,
Marquise de Sévigné

The greatest good you can do for another is not just share your riches but to reveal to him his own.

— Benjamin Disraeli

When friends stop being frank and useful to each other, the whole world loses some of its radiance.

— Anatole Broyard

Forsake not an old friend; for the new is not comparable to him: A new friend is as new wine; when it is old, thou shalt drink it with pleasure.

— Sirach (Apocrypha), chapter 9

The friend who is a helper all the time,
The friend in happiness and sorrow both
The friend who gives advice that is always good,
The friend who has full sympathy with you,
These four the wise see as good-hearted friends
And with devotion cherish such as these
As does a mother cherish her own child.

— Digha Nikaya III.187, Sigalovada Sutta

The only service a friend can really render is to keep up your courage by holding up to you a mirror in which you can see a noble image of yourself.

— George Bernard Shaw

The only reward of virtue is virtue; the only way to have a friend is to be one.

— Ralph Waldo Emerson

Sometimes our light goes out, but it is blown into flame by another human being. Each of us owes deepest thanks to those who have rekindled this light.

— Albert Schweitzer

Treat people as if they were what they ought to be and you help them to become what they are capable of being.

— Goëthe

 Be a Good Friend

1. Talk to your friends — and listen in equal measure.
2. Identify with your friends; empathy is an essential ingredient for friendship.
3. Be trustworthy and loyal; never betray a confidence.
4. Tell your friends how much you care.
5. Show your friends how much you care.
6. Respect and appreciate your differences.
7. Remember that your friend is not a mind reader — and neither are you.
8. If your friend has done something worthy of praise, say so.
9. A healthy friendship is one in which friends are equals.
10. Laugh together.

Friendship is always a sweet responsibility, never an opportunity.

— Kahlil Gibran

Cherish your friend, keep faith in him.

— Sirach 27:17

Sometimes being a friend means mastering the art of timing. There is a time for silence. A time to let go and allow people to hurl themselves into their own destiny. And a time to prepare to pick up the pieces when it's all over.

— Octavia Butler

That is the happiest conversation, where there is no competition, no vanity, but a calm, quiet interchange of sentiments.

— Samuel Johnson

In prosperity our friends know us; in adversity we know our friends.

— John Churton Collins

Enjoying the joys of others and suffering with them — these are the best guides for man.

— Albert Einstein

Offend me and I will question you; this is the medicine for friendship.

— Yoruba proverb

We must love one another or die.

— W. H. Auden

A friend ought always to do good to a friend and never evil.

— Plato

It's the friends you can call up at 4 A.M. that matter.

— Marlene Dietrich

It's Hard to Find a Friend . . .

Rocker Tom Petty could have been talking about making new friends when he wrote those words. But every so often, someone crosses your path and ignites a little spark that says: This could be a friend. Remember, though, that it takes time and sharing to turn acquaintances into friends. The transition from acquaintance to friend is usually a slow, gradual process because friendship, like any intimate relationship, can't be rushed, or forced, into creation; it must be built on shared experience, one shared memory at a time. Yet a new, true friend is always worth the time and effort. So reach out; reveal something of yourself. Take the chance. Spend an hour or two together in a good bookstore — few things tell you more about a person than literary tastes.

Wishing to be friends is quick work, but friendship is slow-ripening fruit.

— Aristotle

In most cases, the transition from acquaintance to friendship occurs gradually. It takes time and effort to build a friendship. They are built slowly, slowly, slowly.... [T]ried-and-true friendships take three years to evolve [and] determine if a friendship has staying power.

— Dr. Jan Yager

Be slow to fall into friendship; but when thou art in, continue firm and constant.

 Just Say Yes

Just like longtime careers or marriages, longtime friendships sometimes lapse into ho-hum routines. If you sense that happening, one way to spice things up is to dip into one of your friend's interests that you've never tried. Go along to the ballet or a baseball game; try water skiing, horseback riding, or tennis, even if you've never thought you'd like it. Maybe it'll turn out that you won't like it. But who knows? You may discover why your friend loves the pastime so much, and you'll dive into it yourself. Either way, both of you will have another memory to carry through the years.

If you're trusted and people will allow you to share their inner garden . . .what better gift?

— Fred Rogers

Be courteous to all but intimate with few, and let those few be well tried before you give them your confidence. True friendship is a plant of slow growth, and must undergo the shocks of adversity before it is entitled to the appellation.

— George Washington

Make new friends but keep the old. One is silver, the other gold.

Anonymous saying, adopted as the Girl Scout motto

We cannot tell the precise moment when friendship is formed. As in filling a vessel drop by drop, there is at last a drop which makes it run over; so in a series of kindnesses there is at last one which makes the heart run over.

— Samuel Johnson

You have to laugh and cry over and over again with someone before you feel comfortable.

— Joan Rivers

A true friend ignores your broken fence and admires your flowers.

— Anonymous

Lend a Helping Hand

Sometimes, when a friend is going through a truly hard time, there's nothing you can do to do to speed things along. But you can ease some of her burden by relieving her of some responsibilities. Here's how:

✳ Look after her kids or pets so she can devote her full attention to the tasks at hand.

✳ Take on some routine chores: Mow the lawn, wash the car, clean the house, shop for groceries.

✳ If she has a regular volunteer job — say, at a church, thrift shop, or senior center — fill in for her.

✳In a case of death or serious illness, offer to notify friends and acquaintances. Then sit down with a phone and your friend's address book and start dialing.

If Your Connection Has Been Broken, Reconnect

It's happened to all of us: Friends move away, our lives change. We promise to stay in touch, and sometimes we do — sort of. Then one day we wake up and realize it's been years since we've even exchanged holiday cards. If you find yourself thinking often of an old friend, stop thinking — pick up the phone and call her. If you don't know where she is, track her down. That's easier than ever these days, thanks to Internet search services. Chances are if your friend has been in your thoughts, you've been in hers as well.

We were young together. We grew old. Our children grew up. But what was between us never changed, though we each changed so much.

— Elbert Hubbard

Friendships, like geraniums, bloom in kitchens.

— Blanche H. Gelfant

Do not protect yourself by a fence but rather by your friends.

— Czech proverb

I use the word friend as the term for the highest state of relationship with me.

— C. T. Butler

A friend is someone who is there for you when he'd rather be anywhere else.

— Len Wein